life
on the land

Translation: Jean Grasso Fitzpatrick

© Parramón Ediciones, S.A.
First Edition, October, 1986
The title of the Spanish edition is *la vida sobre la tierra*

All inquiries should be addressed to:
Barron's Educational Series, Inc.
250 Wireless Boulevard
Hauppauge, New York 11788

Library of Congress Catalog Card No. 87-12545

International Standard Book No. 0-8120-3864-9

Library of Congress Cataloging-in-Publication Data
Rius, María.
   Life on the land.

   (Habitats)
   Translation of: La vida sobre la tierra.
   Summary: A tall tree in a forest explains to a tiny
tree about how plants and animals are nourished and are
dependent on each other. Includes factual information
on plants and their importance to people.
   [1. Trees — Fiction. 2. Forest ecology — Fiction.
3. Ecology — Fiction]   I. Parramón, José María.
II. Title.   III. Series: Rius, María. Habitats.
PZ7.R5213Lk   1987   [E]   87-12545
ISBN 0-8120-3864-9

Legal Deposit: B-41.001-87

Printed in Spain by Cayfosa
Sta. Perpètua de Mogoda
(Barcelona)

7 8 9   9960   9 8 7 6 5 4 3 2

habitats

life
on the land

María Rius
J. M. Parramón

BARRON'S
New York • Toronto • Sydney

Once upon a time there was a tiny tree.

The tree had been planted in a flowerpot inside the house. It didn't get much light, and it felt very sad.

But one day the children who lived in
the house celebrated Arbor Day. They
brought the tiny tree to school. Their
teacher took them for a walk …

… to the forest. There they planted the tiny tree.

The forest was a huge place. There were giant trees, many plants, and many animals, too. So the tiny tree felt very frightened.

"Frightened? Of what?" asked the tall tree next to it. "The forest is such a wonderful world!" And then the tall tree told the tiny tree all about life in the forest.

"Do you see the sun?" asked the tall tree, looking up toward the sky. "Everything begins with the sun. We couldn't live without it."

"All the plants and flowers – the lilies, violets, ferns, daisies, and the trees like us – need the sun, just the way people need food. Do you see how that vine is climbing up to reach the sunlight?"

"Some animals get their food by eating plants. They eat stalks, and they eat fruit. Do you see that squirrel nibbling on pine nuts and acorns? And look at that rabbit eating grass!"

"There are also animals in the forest that eat other animals – like the bear and the wolf. Even the birds eat worms!"

"There are hundreds of birds," said the tall tree. "Some live in our highest branches – like the owl. Others, like the robin and the woodpecker, prefer the low branches."

"And there are thousands of insects! Just take a look and you can see them everywhere – beetles, butterflies, bees, dragonflies, caterpillars."

"And look at the ground in the forest! All you can see are soggy leaves, but underneath there are mushrooms, mosses, and germs that feed the plants and bushes and trees – even you and me."

"Some children planted you, remember?
Children love the forest, and they learn
so much in it. There are so many
wonderful things in the forest!
THIS IS LIFE ON THE LAND!"